Localities

...in...

ANCIENT DOVER.

In the interest of creating a more extensive selection of rare historical book reprints, we have chosen to reproduce this title even though it may possibly have occasional imperfections such as missing and blurred pages, missing text, poor pictures, markings, dark backgrounds and other reproduction issues beyond our control. Because this work is culturally important, we have made it available as a part of our commitment to protecting, preserving and promoting the world's literature. Thank you for your understanding.

LOCALITIES

IN

ANCIENT DOVER.

BY JOHN R. HAM, M.D.

Concord, N. H.:
PRINTED BY THE REPUBLICAN PRESS ASSOCIATION.
1887.

LOCALITIES.

The town of Dover, N. H., originally embraced within its limits the present towns of Somersworth, Rollinsford, Newington, Madbury, Durham, and Lee. The land in the town was voted to the settlers from time to time in public town-meeting, held in the old meeting-house on Dover Neck. These grants of land were from ten to four hundred acres each, and were laid out by the lot-layers, chosen in annual town-meeting. The record of the surveys and bounds of these grants made by the lot-layers, now a part of Dover town records, furnishes the names by which some of the localities were called in the infancy of the settlement. The common lands of the town were divided among the inhabitants in 1732, and the land grants by the town ceased.

ASH SWAMP (THE). There was an ash swamp, so called as early as 1694, between Nock's marsh and Barbadoes pond, and another between Salmon Falls and Cochecho.

BACK RIVER. This name is found in these land grants as early as 1649, and was given to the stream which flows into the Pascataqua river on the west side of Dover Neck. The settlers gave the name to the stream from its mouth up to the head of tide-water, where Sawyer's Woollen Mills now stand; above tide-water at the first falls it became Belleman's Bank river, and now called Bellamy river.

BARBADOES POND. On the Littleworth road, four miles from the city hall, and lying in the present town of Madbury. It was so called as early as 1693, and "commonly so called" in 1701. Is it not the same as "Turtle" pond, which is mentioned in a land grant in 1719? The name is retained to this day.

BARBADOES SPRING. The spring lying south of the pond, and which supplies the south side of Dover with water, was thus called as early as 1701.

BARBADOES SWAMP. So called in 1693, and also called the Ash swamp. It lay south of the pond of the same name.

BEACH HILL. It was "commonly so called" in 1652, and is the long hill, partly in Madbury and partly in Durham, which lies near and to the south-west of Hicks's hill, and just south of the road leading from Hicks's hill to Lee. At the west end was an Indian burial-ground, and in 1652 it was spoken of as "att yᵉ Indian graves, att Beach Hill."

BEARD'S CREEK. So called as early as 1672. It is the brook which flows into Oyster river on the north side, next below the falls of the same.

BEAVER DAM (THE GREAT). In 1659 Capt. Thomas Wiggin had a grant of land "neare yᵉ Great Beaver

Dam. on y*e* south branch of Bellomans Bank river," and the name is retained in land grants down to 1720. The "Beaver Pond Meaddow" was mentioned in 1693. It was one quarter of a mile above the confluence of the Mallego and Belloman's Bank rivers. Where was the Little Beaver Dam, whose existence is implied in the above title?

BELLAMY. A locality and a river. As a locality, the neighborhood about the falls lately occupied by William Hale. As a river, the whole river upon which are Sawyer's mills, from its source down as far as tide-water; below the head of tide-water it becomes Back river. For the origin of the name, see "Belleman's Bank."

BELLEMAN'S BANK. The steep bank on the north side of the stream now known as Bellamy river, near Dunn's bridge at Sawyer's upper mill. The stream is often mentioned in the early land grants as "the freshett that flows past Belleman's Bank." The origin of this name has always baffled those who are curious in such matters, and the correct solution, as we think, is now for the first time offered.

A deed on the old Norfolk Co., Mass., records, shows that "Mr." William Bellew owned a house and twenty acres of land on the north side of the stream in 1644, and that he sold it to Christopher Lawson. And in 1648, when the "Great Cochecho marsh" was divided among the settlers, we find one lot set apart "for Mr. William Belley"—denoting that he, although absent, yet had interests here. The prefix of distinction shows him to have been a man of good position. We find him in Oyster River parish (now the town of Durham), in 1647, as a witness to a deed given by Darby Field, and he signed his name WILL: BELLEW.

If Mr. William Bellew, or "Belley," was absent, and some man in his employ occupied his premises at the Bank above mentioned, then the occupant would be, in common parlance, "Mr. Belley's man," which corresponds with other similar cases on the Dover records. And the bank, on which these premises were situated, would easily be designated as "Mr. Belley's Man's Bank." The ready contraction of these names into "Belleman's Bank" was natural. It became "Bellamy" Bank at about 1800, and afterwards the name, which had become applied to that entire neighborhood, became restricted to the locality above the original bank, where Mr. William Hale, now of Dover, purchased, who at once dropped the word "Bank" from the name, and simply called the locality, and the stream, Bellamy.

BELLEMAN'S BANK RIVER. So called as early as 1646, in land grants. It is the stream which becomes Back river at the head of tide-water, at Sawyer's Woollen Mills. The settlers always applied the name to the fresh water part of the stream above the falls; Back river was always used by them to indicate the stream below the falls at the head of tide-water.

It is written in the land grants, Belleman's bank, Beleman's bank, Belliman's bank, Beliman's bank, Belloman's bank, Bellomay bank, Belemye bank, and Bellemie bank. And in the later town records, from about the year 1800 to 1840, it is written Bellamy bank.

When Mr. William Hale, now of Dover, purchased the land and falls next above Sawyer's mills, he at once dropped the word "bank" from the locality and from the stream, and they are now known as "Bellamy." For the origin of the name, see Belleman's Bank.

BLACK WATER. A locality so called as early as 1693. It lies north of Cochecho pond, and the brook running through it is called Blackwater brook.

BLIND WILL'S NECK. Blind Will, a sagamore of the Indians about Cochecho, was a friendly Indian in the service of Major Richard Waldron. In March, 1677, Major Waldron sent out eight friendly Indians to obtain information as to the presence of hostile Indians. This party was surprised by a band of Mohawks, and only two or three escaped. Blind Will was dragged away by the hair, and, being wounded, perished on the neck of land at the confluence of the Isinglass and Cochecho rivers. This neck has ever since been called Blind Will's Neck.

BLOODY POINT. The point of land in Newington opposite Dover Point. The name arose, in 1631, from a *bloodless* dispute, as to the jurisdiction of the spot, between Capt. Walter Neal, the agent of the Portsmouth settlement, and Capt. Thomas Wiggin, the agent of the Dover settlement. The name came at length to denote all of Dover's territory on the south side of the Pascataqua river, and is retained as the name of the point to this day. Whitehouse's map of Dover, in 1834, has *incorrectly* placed Bloody Point on the north side of the Pascataqua, viz., on Dover Neck.

BRANSON'S CREEK. This name was given as early as 1653 to a tributary on the western side of Oyster river, near its mouth.

BRISTOL. On an old map, in 1634, the settlement at (now) Dover was called Bristol.

BUNKER'S CREEK. It flows into Oyster river, eastern side, and is near the Bunker garrison.

BUNKER'S GARRISON. Bunker's garrison, which was successfully defended in the Indian massacre at Oyster river, on July 17, 1694, and which stands to-day in an excellent state of preservation, is on the east side of the river, on the road leading from the mouth to the first falls.

CALVES PASTURE (THE). The name given to a town pasture as early as 1652, when it was laid out. It was on Dover Neck, bordering on Back river, and contained thirty-six acres in 1722, when it was divided among the settlers.

CAMPIN'S ROCKS. This name was given as early as 1660 to a high granite ledge on the western bank of the Cochecho river, about a mile below the first falls, and which by projecting into the river constitutes the "Narrows." Tradition says a man named Campin, being pursued by Indians, was obliged to jump from the ledge into the river in order to escape.

CAMPRON RIVER. This name was given, as early as 1647, to what was afterwards called the Lamper-eel river, and now the Lamprey river.

CEDAR POINT. So called in 1652. It is the point of land on the west of the mouth of Back river, and lies north of Goat island.

CHARLES'S POINT. This name was given, as early as 1660, to a point at the entrance of Little bay, in Oyster River parish. From Charles Adams, who lived near here.

CLAY POINT. A point of land on the east side of Dover Neck, and so called as early as 1656.

COCHECHO. The Indian name of the *falls* on the river, where the city of Dover now stands. It was spelled by the first settlers in various ways, viz., Cutt-che-choe, Co-che-cha, and Cochecho. The settlers applied the Indian name of the *falls* to the *stream* which flows over the falls and which is lost in the Newichawannock at Cochecho Point, and also to the *settlement* clustered about the falls. It is retained as the name of the stream to this day. The error of the engrossing clerk of the N. H. legislature gave the manufacturing company that built the Dover Cotton Mill the title *Cocheco M'f'g Co.*, instead of *Cochecho*.

COCHECHO GREAT HILL. So called as early as 1659, and is what is now commonly, but erroneously, called Garrison Hill. See "Great Hill."

COCHECHO LOG SWAMP. Thus named as early as 1659; it was between Cochecho and Belloman's Bank rivers, and above tide-water. There are good reasons for thinking it was also called "Capt. Waldron's Logging Swamp," which see.

COCHECHO MARSH. Sometimes called Cochecho Fresh Marsh. It was thus named as early as 1648, when it was surveyed and cut up into lots, and divided among the settlers. It was immediately north of the "Great Hill at Cochecho." The "cartway" which led to it was laid out as early as 1648, and is now the Garrison Hill road. The "Half-way Swamp" was on the south of the "Great Hill," on the opposite side of the "cartway" from said hill.

COCHECHO POINT. So called as early as 1655. The point of land between the Cochecho and Newichawannock rivers, at their confluence.

COCHECHO POND, or "The pond att Cochecho." This pond was thus named as early as 1674; and as early as 1650 it was called "the great pond" in the land grants. It retains its name on all Dover maps, except the Hitchcock County Atlas of 1871. It is now commonly called Willand's pond, from two generations of Willand's who resided at the head of it.

COCHECHO RIVER. The river on which the city of Dover stands, and which flows into the Newichawannock at Cochecho Point.

COFFIN'S GARRISON. On the 28th of June, 1689, Peter Coffin had a garrison on what is now Central avenue, Dover, and between Orchard and Waldron streets. It was taken in the Indian assault on Cochecho on the above date.

Peter's son, Tristram Coffin, on the same date, had a garrison on the high ground in the neighborhood of the Belknap grammar school-house on Silver street, which he successfully defended at the time of the massacre.

COMMON (THE). There was one on Dover Neck as early as 1649; another was laid out, in 1654, on the point between Fresh creek and the Cochecho river; and another was laid out, in 1675, comprising "all the land above Little John's creek, and west of the path that goes to Belomye Bank to be a common forever." The name, soon after 1675, came to embrace all the ungranted lands in the town, which lands were divided among the inhabitants in 1732.

CURRIAL POINT. So called as early as 1720, and it was situated between St. Albon's cove and Quampheagan, on the west side of the Newichawannock river.

DAME'S POINT. The point between Fresh creek and Cochecho river, at their confluence. Dea. John Dame had the first grant there.

DIRTY BROOK. So called as early as 1694; it flowed into Oyster river, near the second falls.

DOMPLINE COVE. So called as early as 1652. It was in Little bay, Newington side. Was it bad spelling for Dumpling? and was it thus shaped?

DOVER. The name given in 1639 to the Hilton Point settlement. When the Rev. Thomas Larkham, who had resided in Northam, England, came to Dover, in 1640, the name of the settlement was changed to Northam; but on his leaving, in 1641, the settlers changed the name back to Dover.

DOVER NECK. The high ridge of land lying between the Newichawannock and Back rivers.

DOVER POINT. The point at the extremity of Dover Neck, formerly Hilton's Point.

DREW GARRISON. It stands half a mile east of the Back River road, and is in a good state of preservation. The date of its erection is unknown, and it is on the farm owned by the late William Plaisted Drew.

EEL WEIR (THE UPPER). Situated in Cochecho river, above Reyner's brook, and so called as early as 1700.

FAGGOTTY HILL. The hill on the road leading from Garrison hill to Cochecho pond. The name was commonly given to the hill some forty years ago; but it is now known by the name of Gage hill.

FRANKFORT. An island in the Pascataqua river, about two miles below Dover Point, and lying near the eastern bank of the stream. It is an elevated gravel knoll, with sides descending precipitously to the water. It has furnished many vessel loads of ballast, and will finally disappear in this manner.

FIELD'S GARRISON. On Field's Plains in 1694, and owned by Lieut. Zacharias Field.

FIELD'S PLAINS. The name given as early as 1680 to the broad, elevated, sandy plain lying on the Back River road, about one mile below the head of tide-water, viz., below Sawyer's mills, and it derived its name from Lieut. Zacharias Field, who had a garrison there as early as 1694.

FIRST CHURCH MEETING-HOUSE. It was erected in 1634, on Dover Neck, a little below the second house, the location of which is well known, and which was one mile above Hilton's Point, now Dover Point. A careful examination of Winthrop's Journal, and of Belknap's History of New Hampshire, makes it evident that the church was organized within a few days "immediately" following Dec. 13, 1638.

FORE RIVER. The name given as early as 1652 to the Newichawannock river which flowed in *front* of the settlement on Dover Neck, and in contradistinction to the river, which, lying *behind* the neck on which was the settlement, was called Back river.

FOX POINT. The name given, as early as 1652, to a point of land on the south side of the Pascataqua, and lying south-west of Goat Island. Little Bay was on the south side of this point, and Broad Cove on the side next Bloody Point. It is the north-west angle of the present town of Newington, where Little Bay and the Pascataqua river join. It is about half a mile long, ending in the river, and forming a prominent headland on that side of the bay. Tradition says the name originated from the use formerly made of this point to snare foxes. "Reynard, being once driven there, could not escape his pursuers without swimming the river or bay, much too wide for his cunning."

FRENCHMAN'S CREEK. This name was given as early as 1656 to a creek running into Back river on the western side. It was the next creek above Royal's Cove.

FRESH CREEK. This name was given as early as 1648 to a tributary of the Cochecho river, which it joins on the eastern side at a point two miles below the city hall. The name is retained until this day.

GAGE HILL. The hill between Garrison hill and Cochecho pond on the Garrison Hill road, and some forty years ago often called Faggoty hill.

GALLOWS HILL. Gallows hill, "commonly so called" in 1699, was a little above the head of tide-water.

GARRISON HILL. The name was first given to the hill which the road ascends at the foot, and west of the present Garrison hill. John Heard's garrison stood on this small hill on the west side of the road. The name was not given to the "Great hill," *alias* the "Great Cochecho hill," *alias* "Varney's hill," until after 1834. There was never a garrison on the latter, which now goes by the name of Garrison hill. Whitehouse's map, in 1834, calls it Varney's hill.

GARRISON HOUSES. There were five garrisons at Cochecho, that is to say where the city of Dover now stands, at the time of the Indian massacre on June 28, 1689. They were John Heard's, Richard Otis's, Richard Waldron's, Peter Coffin's, and Tristram Coffin's. It is doubtful whether Thomas Paine's house, on now Portland street, was or was not fortified. In other parts of the present city of Dover were John Gerrish's at Belloman's Bank river, as early as 1689; Lieut. Zacharias Field's on Field's Plain, as early as 1694; Clement Meserve's at Back river, now tumbling down; Drew's at Back river, which is in an excellent state of preservation; Pinkham's at Dover Neck, which was said to have been fortified, and which was taken down in 1825; and Lieut. Jonathan Hay's at Tolend, which was pulled down in about 1810.

In Oyster River parish, in 1694, there were twelve garrisons which Belknap mentions, and afterwards there was another near the second falls of Oyster river. In the present town of Lee there were at least two garrisons,—one near the Cartland farm, and Randall's near the Hale farm, which has been taken down recently.

GERRISH GARRISON. Capt. John Gerrish had a garrison at Belloman's Bank river, probably near his mill, which he successfully defended in the Indian massacre at Cochecho on June 28, 1689.

GERRISH'S MILL. Capt. John Gerrish's mill was on Belloman's Bank river, one mile below the forks of the same, and north-west of Barbadoes pond, where the road crosses the stream.

GOAT ISLAND. The large island in Pascataqua river, and so called as early as 1652, lying a little to the west of the mouth of Back river, and just below the mouth of Little Bay, near to the Durham shore. It was granted in 1652 to Lieut. William Pomfrett, and he conveyed it as a gift to his grandson William, the son of Deacon John Dame. When the Pascataqua bridge was built, in 1794, from Durham to Newington, the road crossed this island.

GODDARD'S CREEK. So called as early as 1660; it was the first creek eastward of Lamprey river, in Durham, and flows into Great Bay. It divided in part the counties of Rockingham and Strafford, until 1870, when the line was set over, and a slice of Strafford county was cut off.

GREAT BAY (THE). The body of water formed by the junction of the Squamscot, Lamprey, and Oyster rivers, and which at the Little Bay becomes the Pascataqua river. The settlers called it the Bay of Pascataquack.

GREAT HILL (THE). The name which was given as early as 1652, to what in 1659 was called "The Cochecho Great Hill," which from 1700 to 1834 was called Varney's hill, and which since 1834 has, commonly but erroneously, been called Garrison hill. Whitehouse's map of Dover in 1834 calls it Varney's hill.

GREAT POND (THE). The name which as early as 1650 was given to the pond, which in 1674 was called Cochecho pond. The latter name is retained on Dover maps to this day; but it is commonly called Willand's pond.

GREENLAND. So called as early as 1696 in land grants, viz., "on the road leading to Greenland." It is the town of that name.

GULF (THE). The name given as early as 1656, to a swell in Cochecho river, just below the head of tide water, and which is retained to this day.

HALF WAY SWAMP (THE). The swamp, so called as early as 1652, lying south and west of Garrison hill, south of Starbuck's brook, and on the left side of the "Cartway" which leads from the falls of the river to the "Great Cochecho Fresh Marsh," which lay just to the north of Garrison hill. It was *half-way* from the falls to the last named marsh, and the "Cartway" of 1652 is the present Garrison Hill road.

HARTFORD'S FERRY. In 1717, Nicholas Hartford opened a ferry between Beck's Slip on Dover Neck and Kittery.

HAYES'S GARRISON. In 1812 the garrison of Lieut. Jonathan Hayes, at the junction of the Tole End road and the cross road that runs to the second falls of the Cochecho, and at the foot of Winkley's hill, was pulled down. Lieut. Jonathan Hayes was born Apr. 17, 1732 and died Apr. 15, 1787.

HAYSTACK (THE). So called in Jonas Binn's grant in 1654. It was near Branson's creek, on the west side of Oyster river, near the mouth of the river. What was it?

HEARD'S GARRISON. Capt. John Heard's garrison, which was successfully defended in the Indian massacre of Cochecho on June 28, 1689, was on the opposite side of the "cartway" leading past the Great Hill. The hill on which it stood is at the foot of the Great Hill, and directly west of the same. The "cartway" is the present Garrison Hill road.

HEROD'S COVE. So called in 1664, and was in Great Bay.

HEROD'S POINT. A point of land, so called as early as 1650, in Dea. John Dam's grant, extending in Great Bay on its south side.

HEROD'S WIGWAM. There was an Indian named Herod who had a wigwam on a point of land of same name, in Great Bay, in 1650. The Dam grant mentions both the point and the wigwam.

HICKS'S HILL. See Mahorimet's hill.

HILTON'S POINT. The point of land at the extremity of Dover Neck, named from Edward Hilton, where the settlement was made in 1623, and which settlement took the name of Dover in 1639. The Indian name of the point was Wecanacohunt, sometimes called Wecohamet and Winnichahannat. Hilton's patent calls it Wecanacohunt. It is now called Dover Point.

HOGSTYE COVE. So called as early as 1652, and it was the west end of the southern boundary of Dover, now of Newington, on Great Bay.

HOGSTYE POINT. A point of land in Newington, so called as early as 1656.

HOOKS. A remarkable turn in Belloman's Bank river, just below the entrance of the Mallego, and so called as early as 1694. The name was also given to a remarkable turn in Lampereel river, just below Wadleigh's falls; it is in the present town of Lee.

HOOK MILLS. There are two hook mills named in the land grants. One was at the hook of the Lampereel river, near Wadleigh's falls, and one near the hook of the Belloman's Bank river. The hook mill on Bellamy river was mentioned as early as 1729.

HOPE HOOD'S POINT. A point of land thus named as early as 1694, on the north side of the "Three Creeks," on the western side of Back River. Tradition says Hope Hood, a Sagamore and famous Indian chief, was buried there. Hope Hood (alias Wahowah), with three other Indians, sold land on January 3, 1687, to Peter Coffin, of Dover, and they called themselves in the conveyance the native proprietors. The deed is recorded at Exeter. In the French and Indian massacre at Salmon Falls, on March 18, 1690, Hope Hood had twenty-five Indians under him, and was allied to a party of twenty-seven French under Sieur Hertel. Thirty settlers were killed and fifty-four captured. Hope Hood was killed (says Mather) in 1690, and the same writer speaks of him as "that memorable tygre, Hope Hood." This point with land adjacent was granted to John Tuttle in 1642, and remained in possession of the family till about 1870. Whitehouse's map in 1834 erroneously calls it Hopewood's Point.

HUCKINS'S GARRISON, in Oyster River parish, east of the Woodman garrison, was destroyed by the Indians, and twenty-one or twenty-two people massacred, in August, 1689.

HUCKLEBERRY HILL. The name given as early as 1658, and which is still retained, to a hill on the Dover

Neck road. It is the long hill which one ascends before reaching the highest elevation on the neck.

HUCKLEBERRY SWAMP. It was the Hilton Point swamp, and was laid out in 1652 as the Ox Pasture.

INDIAN BROOK. The brook which flows into Cochecho river on the eastern side, and next above the fourth falls of the same. The name was used as early as 1701 (Varney grant), and its origin is unknown. It crosses the "Scatterwit" road, and runs through the farm of Alderman Nathaniel Horne.

INDIAN CORN GROUND. A tract of land lying between Tole End and Barbadoes pond, and thus called as early as 1693, from which the settlers had land grants from time to time. Probably used by the Indians for cultivating their corn prior to the settlement.

INDIAN GRAVES. A locality on the west end of Beach hill, in the northeast corner of the town of Durham, and so called as early as 1652. In that year Philip Chesley had a grant of land from the town containing seventy-eight acres, "att ye Indian Graves," and in 1715 the Lot Layers resurveyed it, and described the bounds as "beginning att the Indian Graves, att Beach Hill, commonly so called."

Another Indian burial-ground, according to a land grant in 1659 to Benjamin Hull, was on the south-west side of Lampereel river, not far west of a mill that stood on the falls, and exactly on the town line between Dover and Exeter, that is, on the town line between the towns of Durham and Newmarket, as it existed till 1870.

INDIGO HILL. A hill in Somersworth, about three fourths of a mile below Great Falls, and so called as early as 1693. A road was laid out in 1720 by the town of Dover, "between Quamphegan and Indigo Hill and beyond into the common." This road ran directly over Indigo hill, and is now closed up at that point. The new road between Salmon Falls and Great Falls leaves the hill on the right hand side between the road and the river.

JOHNSON'S CREEK. This name was given as early as 1652 to a brook which flows into Oyster river on the eastern side and next above Bunker's creek. Thomas Johnson had a land grant there, and the stream perpetuates his name.

KNIGHT'S FERRY. The old ferry tween Dover Point and Bloody Point.

LAMPEREEL RIVER. So called as early as 1650, when Chris. Lawson and George Barlow had permission from the town of Exeter to set up a saw-mill at Lampereel river, "a little above the wigwams;" but prior to this date, in 1647, it was called Campron river, and Elders Starbuck and Nutter of the Dover church had sawmills on the first falls, where the cotton mills of Newmarket now stand. The Indian name of the first falls was Pascassick, sometimes written Piscassick, and again Puscassick. One of the western branches is now called the Piscassick. The stream is now called Lamprey river.

LITTLE JOHN'S CREEK. Little John was an Indian, and his name was given as early as 1654 to the only brook that crosses the Dover Neck road which requires a bridge. It is below the Wingate farm, and is about two miles below the city hall. It is a tributary of Back River, on the eastern side, and the tide flows up the brook under the bridge in the highway. Joseph Austin had a mill on it in 1658. Whitehouse's map of 1834 calls it Varney's creek.

LITTLEWORTH. The district on the road leading to Barbadoes pond was so called as early as 1724, and is retained till this day. Whitehouse, on his map in 1834, changed the name to Trueworth to suit himself. It is needless to say that no other individual ever called it by that name, nor ever will do so.

LOG HILL. The steep bank where the Dover & Portsmouth Railroad crosses the old bed of the Cochecho river. It was the terminus of the path leading from the "Logging swamp" of Major Richard Waldron, where the logs were tumbled down the bank into the mill-pond.

LONG CREEK. It flows into Great Bay on the north side, and between Durham Point and the mouth of Lamprey river.

LONG HILL lies about a mile and a half north-west of Cochecho pond.

LITTLE BAY. The contraction of Great Bay at the eastern end, from whence issues the Pascataqua river.

LONG POINT. So called as early as 1656. It projects into Great Bay on the south side.

LUBBERLAND. A locality in Durham bordering on Great Bay, and so called as early as 1674. The attempt to show that this is bad spelling for Loverland is a failure. The old grants use the name again and again, and always Lubberland.

MADBURY. A locality so named as early as 1694, and now incorporated as the town of Madbury. The origin of the name is unknown.

MAHORIMET. An Indian sagamore who lived in the limits of the old town of Dover. Samuel Symonds had a grant of 640 acres of land from the general court of Massachusetts, lying on both sides of the "Upper or Island falls" of Lampereel river, now Wadleigh's falls. This land was taken possession of by Symonds on June 3, 1657, "in the presence and by consent of Mahorimet, the sagamore of those parts." The hill in now Madbury was called after him, "Mahorimet's hill," till about 1725, when Joseph Hicks bought land there, and the title subsequently became "Hicks hill."

MAHORIMET'S HILL. This Indian name was perpetuated by the settlers; we find it in constant use from 1660 to 1725. It lies in Madbury, and is now called Hicks's hill, from Joseph Hicks who bought land and resided there from 1720.

MAHORIMET'S MARSH. So called as early as 1661, and for many years after. It was adjacent to Mahorimet's hill, and was probably the low ground immediately to the south and west of the same.

MALLEGO. The north branch of Bellamy Bank river, and was thus named as early as 1659. It arises from Cate's pond in Barrington, and joins Bellamy Bank river in the town of Madbury.

MAST PATH (THE GREAT). There were mast paths in various parts of the town, but the one named above was what is now the road to Littleworth.

MESERVE'S GARRISON. Clement Meserve's garrison, now on land

owned by Gerrish P. Drew, is on the west side of the Back River road, and is in a very dilapidated state.

MOOT, MOOET, OR MOET. Bad spelling for moat, and so called as early as 1656 from its resemblance to the moat or ditch which surrounded old castles. It was applied to a morass in Oyster River parish on the Great Bay, and served to mark the bounds of certain land grants. "The little brook that cometh out of the mooet" is mentioned.

MOUNT SORROWFUL. So called in 1702, when Paul Wentworth had a grant of land there.

"MUCH-A-DOE." The road leading from Dover to "Much-a-doe" is mentioned in a conveyance in 1672. Muchado is a hill in Barrington, and the road referred to was, of course, the Tole-End road.

NARROWS (THE). The narrow channel in Cochecho river, about one mile below the first falls. See Campin's Rocks.

NEEDOM'S POINT. This was so called as early as 1674, and was on Great Bay in Oyster River parish. Nicholas Needham was a member of the Exeter combination in 1638, and the point must have been named for him.

NEWICHAWANNOCK. The Indian name of the *falls* where the Berwick ("Great Works") river enters the (now) Newichawannock river. But the settlers applied the name to the *stream* from Quamphagan (Salmon Falls) to Hilton's Point, where it flows into the Pascatăqua river; and this is the Newichawannock of to-day. The settlers also called it the "Fore River." See Quamphagan and Fore River.

NEWTOWN. So called as early as 1694, and the name is retained to this day. It is in the present town of Lee, about three miles north-west of Hicks's hill.

NOCK'S MARSH. The grant of land to Thomas Nock in 1659, lying on the north side of Belloman's Bank river, about one mile above tide water. In 1659 William Hackett had thirty acres of land "between the path that led from Belloman's Bank to Cochecho," on the south, with the freshitt (river) on the west, and the land of Thomas Nock on the north. The spelling has been changed to Knox marsh by those who have forgotten the name of the original settler.

NORTHAM. When the Rev. Thomas Larkham, formerly of Northam, England, came in 1640 to the pastorate of the First Church, Dover, the settlers changed the name of the town from Dover to Northam; but when Rev. Mr. Larkham left the town in 1641, the former name of Dover was again adopted.

OTIS'S GARRISON. Richard Otis's garrison, which was destroyed on June 28, 1689, in the Indian massacre at Cochecho, stood on the west side of Central avenue on the top of the hill, which is half way from the falls of Cochecho to the "Great Hill." Drake's Book of the Indians and the Otis Genealogy erroneously place the garrison on the east side of (now) Central Avenue. Otis's house in 1655 was on the east side of "the cartway," now Central Avenue; but the land grant was resurveyed to Richard Waldron after the desolation of Cochecho, and it confirms the tradition that the garrison of Otis in

1689 was on the west side of the "cartway," now Central Avenue.

OX PASTURE (THE). It was laid out as such in the Hilton Point swamp in 1652, and was divided among the inhabitants, with other common lands, in 1732.

OYSTER BED. The settlers discovered a bed of oysters in the stream, which, from this circumstance, they called Oyster river. It was half way between the mouth of the river and the first falls of the same.

OYSTER POINT. On one side of the mouth of Thomas Johnson's creek, on the east side of Oyster river, and was so named as early as 1654.

OYSTER RIVER. So called as early as 1640 from the discovery of a bed of oysters half way between the mouth and the first falls of the river. The settlers gave the name to both the stream and the settlement upon it. The parish of Oyster River was included in the limits of Dover till its separate incorporation in 1736 as the town of Durham.

PACKER'S FALLS. The fourth falls in the Lampereel river, in Durham, was granted to Thomas Packer in about 1750. The second and third falls also are now included in "Packer's falls."

PAINE'S GARRISON. In the Indian massacre at Cochecho, on June 28, 1689, Thomas Paine had a house on the road leading from Cochecho to Salmon Falls, now Portland street, at the intersection of Rogers street. Belknap did not mention it in his account of the massacre. It is doubtful if it was or was not fortified.

PAQUAMEHOOD. In 1665, James Paquamehood, an Indian "of Tole End," sold to James Rawlings "three ponds and three hills, with all enclosed lands and marshes." The deed is recorded at Exeter.

PASCATAQUA. (One water parting into three.) The Indian name of the junction of the waters at Hilton's Point. The settlers gave this name to the stream issuing from Little Bay, above Goat island, and which, receiving Back river on the west of Dover Neck, and Newichawannock on the east of Dover Neck, is lost in the sea at Portsmouth. Early historians also gave the name to the settlements upon the stream. The river is now commonly, but erroneously, called Piscataqua.

PASCATAQUACK. The early name of the Great Bay.

PASCASSICK. The Indian name of the first falls of Lamprey river, at the head of tide water, where the cotton mills of Newmarket now stand, and which name the settlers also gave to the western branch of the river. Sometimes Piscassick, sometimes Puscassick, in the land grants. The western branch of Lamprey river is now commonly called Piscassick.

PINE HILL. The hill on which the third meeting-house of First church, Dover, was built before July 16, 1713, and where the dust of the fathers has mouldered for generations, was called Pine Hill as early as 1731.

PINE POINT. A locality in Newington, thus named as early as 1664; another Pine Point was on the Newichawannock, in 1693, just below St. Albons cove.

PINKHAM'S GARRISON. It was on Dover Neck, about half a mile below the second meeting-house lot, and was taken down in about 1825.

PLUM PUDDING HILL. So called in the Coffin grant in 1670; it was between Cochecho and Tole End, on the Tole End road. It was probably the high ground between (now) Lexington and Arch streets.

POMEROY'S COVE. It was on the Newichawannock river; Major Richard Waldron, in 1652, had a grant of Pomeroy's cove "to make a dock." Sandy point bounded it on one side.

QUAKER PASTURES. There were two Quaker Pastures set apart "to the inhabitants of this town [Dover] commonly called Quakers for the better Inabling them to accomodate their Travelling friends." One was voted on May 20, 1717, of ten acres, "by the way that goes to Mallego, at the head of our town bounds between Belleman's Bank river and the mast path that now goeth to Mallego." The other, of ten acres also, was voted in same terms on 25 June, 1717, on Dover Neck, "between the watering gutt and Cochecho."

QUAMPHEGAN OR QUAMPEAGAN. The Indian name of the falls at South Berwick at the head of tide water. The settlers called the stream below the falls the Newichawannock, and the stream above the fall the Salmon Falls river.

REDDING'S POINT. So called as early as 1652; it was a point of land on the south side of the Pascataqua river, east of Goat island.

REYNER'S BROOK. The brook which flows into Cochecho river on the east side, and next above the fifth falls of the same. It derived its name from a grant of land, in 1656, to Rev. John Reyner, and is retained to this day. His grant, comprising 400 acres, was on the east side of Cochecho river, commencing at the upper side of the farm now the homestead of Alderman Nathaniel Horne, and "running northeast from the river 320 rods; thence north-west 240 rods; thence south-west 320 rods to the river, just below the Sunken island; then 240 rods by the river to the first bound." See Sunken island. This grant was relaid to John Waldron in 1721.

RIALL'S COVE. The cove on the western side of Back river, and next south of Frenchman's creek. It was so called as early as 1643. It is the same as Royall's cove, from Teague Riall, or Royall, who had a grant there.

ROADS. On 27 October, 1653, the highway was laid out, five rods wide, from the second falls of the Cochecho "eastward to the swamp." That is from the (now) Whittier's fall to the George W. Page farm. In 1661 a road was laid out from Cochecho to Oyster river, "fitt for man and horse." In 1724 the road was laid out, four rods wide, from Hilton's point to the meeting-house at Pine hill. It was only a narrow cartway prior to this date, and had never been laid out by the town.

ROCK ISLAND. The small island south-east of Goat island, and it was crossed by the Pascataqua bridge of 1794.

ROCKY POINT. The point of land extending from the Newington shore, in Broad cove, and below Fox point, so called as early as 1657. Was this the same as Rock island?

ROYALL'S COVE. It was on the west side of Back river next south of Frenchman's creek, and so called as early as 1643. The same as Riall's cove, from Teague Riall, or Royall, who had a grant of land there.

SANDY BANK. A locality on the east bank of Lamprey river, and so called in the Hugh Donn grant in 1664.

SANDY POINT. On one side of Pomeroy's cove in 1660.

SCATTERWIT. A district on the east side of Cochecho river, adjacent to the fourth falls of the same, and thus called as early as 1701. The Sanford and Everts map of Strafford Co., in 1871, erroneously calls it Scatterwith.

SCOUDEW'S WIGWAM. Philip Scoudew, an Indian, had a grant from the town of marsh land at Great bay prior to 1643, and had a wigwam there in that year.

SHANKHASSICK. The Indian name of the first falls on Oyster river, at the head of tide water.

SLIGO. A district on the west side of the Newichawannock river, lying between St. Albon's cove and Quamphegan, and thus called as early as 1694. Some of the early settlers at this point came from Sligo, Ireland.

SLIGO GARRISON. There was a garrison at Sligo as early as 1709, between St. Albon's cove and Quamphegan.

STARBUCK'S BROOK. The first brook which flows into the Cochecho on the east side, above the first falls of the same. Elder Edward Starbuck had a grant in 1643 at (now) Horne's hill on Sixth street, and the brook at the foot of Horne's hill derived its name from him. Starbuck sold this grant to William Horne, the first of the name in Dover.

STEVENSON'S CREEK. It was thus called as early as 1700, and flows into Oyster river on the south side, below the first falls.

ST. ALBON'S COVE. Situated on the west side of the Newichawannock river, and about one half a mile below the falls at Quamphegan, the head of tide water. It was thus called as early as 1652; it is often called Styles's cove, and is in the town of Rollinsford.

STONY BROOK. Three of the name are mentioned in the land grants, and all of them in the Oyster River parish. One, so called in 1653, in Davis grant, flowed on the south side of the Woodman garrison, and emptied into Beard's creek, on the western side of the same.

Another, so called in 1674, flowed into Oyster river on the south side, and more than a mile below the first falls. The third, mentioned in Doe grant in 1711, flowed into Lampereel river on the east side, and a little below the head of tide water.

SUNKEN ISLAND. An island which has been all under water since the erection of the dam on the fifth falls of the Cochecho, and which was thus called as early as 1700. It is opposite the mouth of the brook which separates the old Dover town farm (now Eli Page's) from the present Strafford county farm. It served in 1721 to mark the west end of the northern line of the 400 acre grant to the Rev. John Reyner, and was thus called in the description of the bounds.

THREE CREEKS (THE). So called as early as 1695, situated near each other, and near the mouth of Back river, on the west side.

TOLE END. A district on the west side of Cochecho river, and adjacent to the second falls of the same, so called, and limited to the second falls in 1658 in the land grants. One grant says, "neare Mr. Towle, his End." A log hill was laid out in 1703, "at the second fall, or Tole End fall," on the west bank. The name has come to be applied to the whole district on the west side of Cochecho river, and lying above the second fall.

TOMSON'S POINT. On the east side of Upper Neck (Dover), and so called as early as 1656.

TURTLE POND. So called in 1694, and again in the Sias grant in 1719, as being "on the north side of the mast path." Was it not another name for Barbadoes pond?

VARNEY'S HILL. The name which, after the purchase of Ebenezer Varney in 1696, was given to the "Great hill," alias the "Great Cochecho hill" From the first grants of land down to 1700 it bore the latter name; from 1700 till since 1834 it was universally called Varney's hill; and since 1834 it has commonly but erroneously been called Garrison hill. Whitehouse's map of Dover, in 1834, calls it Varney's hill.

WADLEIGH'S FALLS. The sixth falls of the Lampereel river, six miles from its mouth, and so called as early as 1701 from the owner, Robert Wadleigh. This fall was called the "Island falls" in a conveyance to Samuel Symonds in 1657, from the fact that an island was in the stream at or near the falls.

WADLEIGH'S MILLS. On the sixth falls of Lampereel river, and so called as early as 1701; also called the "Hook mill," from a remarkable turn in the river near this point.

WALDRON BURIAL GROUND. The burial ground adjoining the Methodist meeting-house. Tradition says the bones of Major Richard Waldron were taken from the smoldering ruins of his garrison in 1689, and buried there. His great-grandson, Capt. Thomas Westbrooke Waldron, who died in 1785, was buried there, and his tombstone says "the remains of Major Richard Waldron lie near this spot."

WALDRON'S GARRISON. Major Richard Waldron's garrison, which was destroyed in the Indian massacre at Cochecho on June 28, 1689, stood on the west side of Central avenue, and midway between First and Second streets, and a few rods back of the present street line. National block stands exactly in front of the garrison site.

WALDRON'S LOGGING SWAMP. In 1652 (then Captain) Richard Waldron had a grant of "two thirds of all the timber lying and growing between Cochecho first falls and Bellemaye Bank, and so westward between the river of Cochecho and the freshitt the runs to Bellomyes Bank to the utmost bounds of Dover." The description of the land grants, and the known location of the Major's mills on the first falls of the Cochecho and the "Log hill" (where the D. & P. R. R. crosses the old bed of the Cochecho), where the logs were tumbled down into the long mill-pond, enables us to locate "the great mast path leading into the logging swamp." It ran from "Log hill" south, in the line of (now) Lexington street, with "Plum Pudding hill" on the immediate right hand side; then curving a little to the west, it crossed "the road leading from Cochecho to Tole

End," and continuing became what is now the road to Littleworth.

WEDNESDAY HILL. So called in land grants as early as 1700; it is in the present town of Lee, a mile and a half south-east of Lee hill, on what was once the Lee town farm, and now owned by Daniel Smith. Tradition says a fight with Indians occurred there on Wednesday, and hence the name of the hill.

WELSHMAN'S COVE. On Great bay in Newington, and was thus called as early as 1652. Did "Welsh" James Grant have land there?

WHEELWRIGHT'S POND. So called from the Rev. John Wheelwright as early as 1666, and the name is retained to this day. It is in the present town of Lee, and is the source of Oyster river. It was at this pond that Captain Wiswall, Lieut. Flagg, Sergeant Walker, and twelve privates were slain, on July 6, 1690, in an engagement with the Indians. Capt. Floyd, with the remainder of the two companies, was obliged to retreat. When Capt. Convers, the next morning, went to look after the wounded, he found the Indians had retreated at the same time. He found seven whites who were wounded, and buried the dead above mentioned.

WHITE HALL. The name of a swamp in Rochester, to the north-east of the Great pond (Cochecho, also Willand's), and so called as early as 1650, when a grant of land was laid out to James Kidd, "north of the Great Pond, on the road leading to White Hall." The name is retained till this day. Was it given as a burlesque on the king's palace of the same name in London?

WILLAND'S POND. The name which is commonly given to what was known as late as 1834, on Whitehouse's map of Dover, as Cochecho pond. The County Atlas of New Hampshire, by Hitchcock, in 1871, calls it Willand's pond. The Strafford County Atlas, by Sanford and Everts, in 1871, calls it Cocheco (*sic*) or Willand's pond. The latter name is derived from a family who lived at the head of the pond.

WINNICHAHANNAT OR WECANACOHUNT. The Indian name of Hilton's point. Edward Hilton's patent, in 1629–'30, March 12, calls it Wecanacohunt; but Capt. Thomas Wiggin, May 22, 1656, surrendered his interest in the "Winnichahannat or Hilton point" lands.

WOODMAN'S GARRISON. Capt. John Woodman's garrison, which was successfully defended in the Indian massacre at Oyster river on July 17, 1694, and which stands to-day in a good state of preservation, is on the east side of Oyster river, and half a mile above the falls at the head of tide water.

Printed by Libri Plureos GmbH in Hamburg,
Germany